Completing the Sales Transactions

Transactions

Workbook 8

D1490202

Completing the Sales Transactions
Workbook 8

CREDITS:

Product Manager:	**Debbie Woodbury**
Production Editor:	**Genevieve McDermott**
Production Artists:	**Nicole Phillips and Rich Lehl**
Manufacturing:	**Julia Coffey**
Advisor:	**Margery Steinberg, Ph.D.**
Cartoonist:	**James McFarlane**

Based on materials developed by Martha B. Moran, Ph.D. and John Donnellan, Ph.D.

COPYRIGHT © 2006 Axzo Press. All Rights Reserved.

No part of this work may be reproduced, transcribed, or used in any form or by any means—graphic, electronic, or mechanical, including photocopying, recording, taping, Web distribution, or information storage and retrieval systems—without the prior written permission of the publisher.

For more information, go to **www.courseilt.com**

For permission to use material from this text or product, submit a request online at: www.thomsonrights.com

Any additional questions about permissions can be submitted by e-mail to: thomsonrights@thomson.com

Trademarks

Crisp Series is a trademark of Axzo Press.

Some of the product names and company names used in this book have been used for identification purposes only and may be trademarks or registered trademarks of their respective manufacturers and sellers.

Disclaimer

We reserves the right to revise this publication and make changes from time to time in its content without notice..

ISBN 10: 1-4239-5074-7
ISBN 13: 978-1-4239-5074-5
Library of Congress Catalog Card Number 99-75997
Printed in the United States of America
3 4 5 12 11 10

Learning Objectives for

COMPLETING THE SALES TRANSACTIONS

The learning objectives for *Completing the Sales Transactions* are listed below. They have been developed to guide the user to the core issues covered in this book.

The objectives of this book are to help the user:

1) Handle transactions and related paperwork

2) Open, maintain, and close the cash register

3) Package merchandise appropriately

4) Assure that shipping/mailing/deliveries are handled properly

Preface

Welcome to the *Crisp Retailing Smarts Series,* designed specifically for the retail sales associate. This series is based on skill standards developed by a team of industry practitioners and educators under the leadership of the National Retail Federation, the world's largest retail association.

The topics covered in these workbooks reflect what employers across the country agree is needed to succeed and grow in a retail career, regardless of the size or nature of the enterprise. The *Crisp Retailing Smarts Series* sets a new standard for industry-driven learning that leads to productive and measurable results and helps prepare candidates for rewarding careers in retail and other service industries.

The skill standards followed here have been developed for the professional sales associate for several reasons:

➤ The majority of North American workers initially enter the workforce through a job in the retail industry. Many choose to make retailing a lifelong career, adding new skills as they progress.

➤ The skills required for success in these entry-level positions are the same skills that will help workers succeed throughout their lives, both personally and professionally, whether in the retail industry or some other field of work or profession.

➤ In our current service-oriented and global economy, organizations must attract and retain a dedicated, competitive workforce. Skills are a key attribute when selecting these workers.

As you use these materials, take advantage of the exercises and self-assessments that will help you better understand the skills and techniques being explained. Studies show that adults retain new skills more effectively if they apply them immediately to their own experiences. After you have completed the reading and activities in each section, look for opportunities to put the lessons into practice. Then use the *Learning Checklist* in the back of the book to record your progress and successes.

We are proud to help the retailing industry pioneer the development of skill standards and raise expectations for a committed and competitive workforce. And we are proud that learners like yourself are taking your future into your own hands and mastering the skills that will bring you success and recognition in your chosen profession.

Tracy Mullin

Tracy Mullin
President and CEO
National Retail Federation

The Finishing Touches

Even after you successfully close a sale, there are still things to be done. Completing the transaction is more than simply handing the customer a receipt and saying, "Have a nice day!" Both your customer and your employer have specific needs and expectations that you must meet if you are to become a professional sales associate.

Each time you complete a transaction, you have several equally important responsibilities. Taking care of customer payment; completing necessary paperwork; keeping accurate records; and coordinating packing, shipping, and delivery of purchases to the customer are all skills that you will need to have. Dealing with these situations with accuracy, efficiency, and enthusiasm will guarantee an employer's faith in your ability and hopefully win the customer's satisfaction and continued patronage!

Table of Contents

Will That

Be Cash?

Will That Be Cash?

All of your hard work in getting to know customers and helping them make the right decisions is about to pay off—literally! This is the point in the sales process when everyone involved needs to be confident that the transaction is being done correctly. Everyone is counting on you and you can master this step with just a few words of advice and a little practice.

The "Register"

The *till,* the *drawer,* the *point-of-sale terminal,* or simply the *register.* Whatever you call it, it is much more than a mere piece of machinery. Some might call the register the heart of the organization, because through it flows the lifeblood of the company—cash (or its equivalent). Others might consider it the brain of the enterprise, because it stores and processes so much information that is vital to the business. For instance, some systems keep track of inventory and tell merchandise buyers when it is time to order more stock. Others allow you to help customers check the status of their special orders, the balance of their accounts, or the record of what they bought in the past.

Of course, we all know that it is really you who are the heart, brain, eyes, ears, mouth, and helpful hands of the store! And that piece of equipment, whether it is a simple cash box or a sophisticated point-of-sale (POS) computer system, depends on you to feed it accurate information so it can work effectively.

Opening... In many retail situations, the sales associate is responsible for "opening" the register. This may include filling the cash drawer with a specific number of bills and coins so you can make change for customers who pay with cash. Obviously, stores need to be very careful with money (and so do you!). Therefore, it is very important that you understand and follow the store's procedures for setting up the register.

You may be required to *sign out* cash. This means counting the money and making sure the amount is correct and recorded carefully. You should double-check this *before you ring up any sales.* This tally will be used to calculate your total sales for the day. If money is missing, you will be held responsible.

Closing... At the end of your shift, you may also be responsible for counting the money and making sure the drawer is *balanced* or *reconciled.* A common way to do this is to calculate the total sales during your shift, using the register tape or an automated process, and comparing that to the amount of money in the cash drawer, minus the original cash put in when the register was opened. Follow your store's procedures carefully whenever you close down the register or when someone replaces you at the terminal. This process is usually called *closing* or *cashing out.*

And everything in between... During your shift, you will make many transactions requiring you to ring up the correct price, total the sale, accept payment from customers, count back change, and put money away for safekeeping. Every store will have unique procedures for this as well as for accepting checks and credit cards (discussed in Lesson 2). But some things are universal, such as the need to read prices carefully and accurately and to win the customer's confidence by being professional and trustworthy.

Things to watch for:

➤ Enter prices carefully and put the decimal point in the right place—there's a BIG difference between $5.00 and $50.

➤ Make sure you are entering the right quantity—everyone loves a "three-for-the-price-of-two special" but no one wants to pay three times for only two items.

➤ If your system asks for item numbers or SKUs, be sure you enter them: this helps keep track of inventory so you won't have to disappoint a later customer by saying, "I'm sorry, we are out of those right now."

➤ Be especially careful if you are entering a customer's account number: nothing will make a customer lose confidence in a store faster than an incorrect bill.

➤ Make sure you are subtracting when you credit a customer with a return and adding when you are processing a purchase.

➤ Don't forget sales tax or any other additional charges.

Technology can be your friend... Today computerized POS terminals do many things that make it easier for you to ring up a sale and save the customer time. This technology, which is being used by both large and small retailers, allows tasks that used to be done by hand to be done now using computers. The computer reduces checkout time and lessens the chance of mistakes in ringing up the sale. Some computer terminals do things like completing shipping forms and preparing gift certificates. These systems can also keep track of what customers are buying, so stores will know what inventory needs to be reordered.

More and more, stores are relying on the use of bar codes on products that are read by the computer by using optical scanners. These scanners may be flat, such as those you see in grocery stores, or handheld, which are used in many specialty and department stores. The bar codes automatically record the current price of the item, including any discounts and taxes.

Barcodes, found on most product packaging, may be used in place of price tags for retailers who use point-of-sale scanners.

Even with all of this technology, it is a good idea to become familiar with the basic processes and procedures, such as how to calculate sales tax. You never know when technology might fail you or you have to review a transaction with a customer to make sure she understands her bill. If your store automatically calculates everything for you, you might ask a co-worker or your manager for a quick lesson in how to do it "the old-fashioned way" just to be prepared!

A QUICK REVIEW OF TERMS

balancing, closing, cashing out, or reconciling— making sure the total amount of cash sales, minus the amount in the drawer, equals the amount of money you started your shift with

inventory—the number of items a store has on hand that are ready to be sold

opening—counting and filling the cash drawer with bills and coins at the beginning of your shift

point-of-sale terminal—the machine on which you ring up sales

signing out cash—counting and recording the amount of money in the cash reigster

Cold, Hard Cash

Keeping it safe... Here is a very important rule: Never place cash directly into the cash drawer before you make change for the customer. When the customer gives you cash, place it on the ledge above the drawer until the transaction is complete. This way there can be no mistake about the amount of money that was given to you by the customer.

Unfortunately, some less-than-honest people will employ a scam in which they claim to have given you a $20 bill, when they actually gave you a $10. If you have already put the $10 bill in the cash drawer, it is your word against theirs if they say you owe them more change. By keeping the money visible, you can simply show them what bill(s) they gave you.

Keeping it straight... When you do finally place money in the register drawer, do it carefully, making sure that the coins and bills are placed in the correct compartments. This will prevent mistakes later as you make change for other customers. Usually larger bills, such as $50 and $100, are placed under the drawer along with checks and credit card receipts.

Tip: *Take the initiative to learn how to spot counterfeit money. Ask your manager or your banker to show you what to look for.*

Keeping it simple... The easiest way to figure the amount of change is to "count up" from the purchase total to the amount of money given to you by the customer. For instance, if the purchase amount is $2 and the customer gives you $5, you put the five-dollar bill on the ledge above the register and, starting mentally with $2, physically take out dollar bills one at a time until you count up to five.

Sales Associate: "Okay, that is $2…"

(then count out dollars) "…3, 4, and 5 makes $5."

Tip: *Show courtesy and respect by always counting change back into the customer's hand. Never lay it on the counter, where it will be difficult for the customer to pick up. If the customer is busy with other things, wait until she is ready to accept her change.*

Here is another example, using coins as well as bills.

The amount due is $5.15. The customer gives you a $10.00 bill.

First, count up to $6.00 as follows:

> 5.15 + .10 (dime) = 5.25
>
> 5.25 + .25 (quarter) = 5.50
>
> 5.50 + .25 = 5.75
>
> 5.75 + .25 = 6.00

Then count up to $10.00:

> 6.00 + 1.00 (dollar) = 7.00
>
> 7.00 + 1.00 = 8.00
>
> 8.00 + 1.00 = 9.00
>
> 9.00 + 1.00 = 10.00

You should count this out first into your own hand from the cash drawer, then repeat it as you count it back into the customer's hand.

You can say: "$5.15 and .10 is $5.25" and as you put each coin or dollar into the customer's hand continue to count up: "$5.50, $5.75, $6.00, $7.00, $8.00, $9.00, and $10.00."

Tip: *The more you handle money, the more comfortable you will be with it. Practice counting back change at home or with a friend.*

NOW YOU FIGURE IT OUT

Calculate the amount of change due to each customer using the count-back method.

The amount due is $21.10 and the customer gives you a twenty-dollar bill and a five-dollar bill. How much change does the customer get back? Add the coins and bills, counting up from $21.10 to $25.00:

$21.10	+	.10	(dime)	=	21.20
$21.20	+	.05	(nickel)	=	21.25
$21.25	+	.25	(quarter)	=	21.50
$21.50	+	.25		=	21.75
$21.75	+	.25		=	22.00
$22.00	+	1.00	(dollar)	=	23.00
$23.00	+	1.00		=	24.00
$24.00	+	1.00		=	25.00

You give the customer: 1 dime, 1 nickel, 3 quarters, and 3 one-dollar bills (see middle column).

CONTINUED

CONTINUED

Now try it yourself:

1. The amount due is $33.17 and the customer gives you $35. What kind of change does the customer receive?

$33.17	+	.01	(penny)	=	33.18
$33.18	+		( )	=	
$33.19	+		( )	=	
$33.20	+		( )	=	
$33.25	+		( )	=	
$33.50	+		( )	=	
$33.75	+		( )	=	
$34.00	+		( )	=	35.00

You give the customer:

2. The amount due is $234.68 and the customer gives you $300.00. What kind of change does the customer receive back?

$234.68	+	( )	=	
$	+	( )	=	
$	+	( )	=	
$	+	( )	=	
$	+	( )	=	
$	+	( )	=	
$	+	( )	=	
$	+	( )	=	300.00

You give the customer:

CONTINUED

═══ CONTINUED ═══

3. The amount due is $51.25 and the customer gives you 3 twenty-dollar bills, 1 one-dollar bill, and 1 quarter.

How much money did the customer give you? _____

What kind of change does the customer receive back? Use the counting-up method.

$ _____ + _____ (_____) = _____

$ _____ + _____ (_____) = _____

$ _____ + _____ (_____) = _____

$ _____ + _____ (_____) = _____

$ _____ + _____ (_____) = _____

$ _____ + _____ (_____) = _____

$ _____ + _____ (_____) = _____

$ _____ + _____ (_____) = _____

You give the customer:

Compare your answers to those in the Appendix.

P A R T 2

Accepting Checks and Credit Cards

Accepting Checks and Credit Cards

While each retailer will have specific rules about accepting personal checks, most will require at least some form of identification from the check-writing customer. Customers expect this, so you don't need to be embarrassed to ask. In fact, most stores will have their check-cashing policy posted where customers can see it. If someone should object, you can explain that the policy is for customers' protection as well as the store's.

Checking in All the Right Places

Checking I.D. ... Your request for identification should be simple and polite. Customers understand that this is just part of your job, but if you are too abrupt or demanding when asking for identification, they may take it personally and not feel like a valued and trusted customer. The reason for requesting identification is to verify that the check actually belongs to that customer. You do this by comparing the name imprinted on the check and the signature to the name and signature on the identification. Usually a driver's license and/or a major credit card is all that is needed. If the customer does not have a driver's license, your store may require some other form of picture I.D.

Checking for completeness... Look to see that the date and the amount (in numbers and written out) are correct. Make sure that the signature and address corresponds to the information on the customer's identification. Your store may request that you record specific information on the check as you are reviewing it. When accepting traveler's checks, you need to witness the customer signing and dating the check. People sign all of their traveler's checks in one place when they first get them from a bank or agency. Then, as they cash these checks, they are to sign them a second time; one of your jobs is to make sure both signatures match.

Personal Check

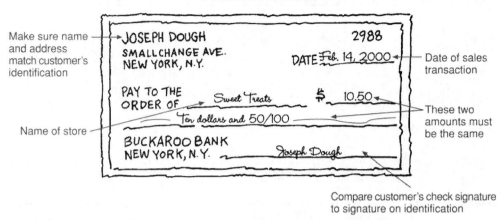

Make sure name and address match customer's identification

Name of store

Date of sales transaction

These two amounts must be the same

Compare customer's check signature to signature on identification

Traveler's Check

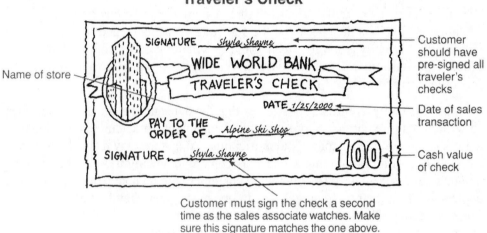

Name of store

Customer should have pre-signed all traveler's checks

Date of sales transaction

Cash value of check

Customer must sign the check a second time as the sales associate watches. Make sure this signature matches the one above.

Check printers... If your company has automatic check printers, you can offer to save customers some time and effort. Customers give you a blank check and you insert it into the machine as you finalize the transaction. The date, the store's name, and the purchase amount will all be printed, and customers only have to sign their name. This makes the check-writing process fast and accurate.

Better than a check... Debit cards replace the need for paper checks altogether. They look like credit cards, but act like checks. Debit cards are issued by banks as an extension of the customer's checking account. Customers either punch a code into a keypad at the point-of-sale terminal or they sign what looks just like a credit card receipt (more on that next). In either case, you need to carefully follow any store policies about checking for identification or providing receipts.

Tip: *Always ask customers if they would like the receipt put in the bag with their items. Some customers prefer to keep their receipts in their wallets or purses.*

Sure, We Take Credit Cards!

The majority of retailers accept credit or debit cards. In fact, 40% to 60% of department and specialty store purchases are on credit. Even some supermarkets and fast-food chains now allow credit or debit card transactions. The major national credit cards are Visa, MasterCard, American Express, and Discover. Be familiar with which cards your store accepts and the steps for using them.

Part of your job is to make sure that the card is still valid by checking the expiration date. You should also watch the customer sign the receipt and compare this signature to the one on the back of the card. Customers will appreciate knowing that you are protecting them as well as the store.

Make sure the credit card is being used by the right person. If a man is using a card issued to a "Mrs." (or vice-versa), you should point out that he may accidentally be using his wife's card and ask for a different card.

Handling rejection... Many credit companies require sales associates to check with them first before completing a credit card transaction. This is usually done electronically by using a special telephone number. When you follow the steps of this process, you will normally be given an authorization number or other form of permission for the charges. However, if there is a problem with the credit account, you may get a code alerting you to special situations.

Some reasons credit card authorization might be denied or questioned:

➤ The customer has exceeded the established credit limit

➤ The card has been reported lost or stolen

➤ The customer has placed certain restrictions on the card's use

➤ The creditor is denying credit due to late payment

When a customer's credit card is rejected, you need to handle the situation courteously and try to spare the customer any undue embarrassment. Inform the customer of the problem; ask if he or she would like to use a different credit card or pay with cash. If you suspect that the credit card is stolen, follow store procedures and know who to ask for help.

Sale Associate: "I'm sorry, I am getting a code from the creditor that says I cannot accept your credit card at this time. Do you have any reason to think that I am getting this code in error?"

Customer: "I have no idea why my card would be rejected. Are you sure?"

Sale Associate: "I will try again if you like, but perhaps you'd prefer to pay with a different card or maybe cash?"

Tip: After you have processed a credit card, lay it signature-side up on the counter near you. This allows you to check the signature as the customer is signing the credit slip.

DO THESE CHECK OUT?

Circle any errors and make a note of any mistakes that a sales associate should notice on the following checks.

```
JOSEPH DOUGH                              2988
SMALL CHANGE AVE.
NEW YORK, N.Y.           DATE  3/17/2000

PAY TO THE
ORDER OF  Shamrock Cafe        $   25.95
          Ten and 95/100

BUCKAROO BANK
NEW YORK, N.Y.              Joseph Dough
```

```
JOSEPH DOUGH                              2988
SMALL CHANGE AVE.
NEW YORK, N.Y.           DATE

PAY TO THE
ORDER OF  Sal's Signs          $   250.00
       Two hundred fifty and no/100

BUCKAROO BANK
NEW YORK, N.Y.              Joseph Dough
```

CONTINUED

CONTINUED

JOSEPH DOUGH   2988
SMALL CHANGE AVE.
NEW YORK, N.Y.   DATE *April 14, 2000*

PAY TO THE
ORDER OF ___*Linda's Oil Lamps*___ $ *10.40*
_____*Ten and 40/100*_____

BUCKAROO BANK
NEW YORK, N.Y.   *Joseph B. Broke*

SIGNATURE ___*Joyce Allen*___

WIDE WORLD BANK

TRAVELER'S CHECK

DATE *June 20, 2000*

PAY TO THE
ORDER OF ___*Cape Cod Rentals*___

SIGNATURE ___*Joyce Allen*___   100

Compare your answers to those in the Appendix.

P A R T 3

Completing

the Paperwork

Completing the Paperwork

In this era of fast food, overnight delivery and facsimile machines, customers are accustomed to speedy service and expect to get through the checkout line quickly."

– Kenneth E. Stone, *Competing with the Retail Giants*

In the not-too-distant past, all of the record keeping for a retail operation was completed manually—sales associates created handwritten receipts for their customers and then wrote a duplicate version for the store's records. These records were then reviewed by the manager to update the inventory list, which in turn was used by the buyer to write orders when it was time to restock merchandise. All of this information was used by the owner or accountant to complete the various financial records such as accounting ledgers, tax statements, and so on.

These processes still exist today, but in large retail organizations much of the handwriting has been replaced by the use of computers. And the analysis of that data has been automated using software programs that put the information into a central database. Even so, many smaller retailers, for whom the computer-based systems would be too costly or otherwise unjustified, still rely on paper-based records. When this is the case, the sales associate must learn not only to complete the paperwork correctly, but also to do it quickly and not keep the customer waiting.

When people wait up to about a minute and a half, their sense of how much time has elapsed is fairly accurate. Anything over 90 or so seconds, however, and their sense of time distorts…If they've waited 2 minutes, they'll say it's been 3 or 4…Having an employee simply acknowledge that the shopper is waiting—and maybe offer some plausible explanation—automatically relieves time anxiety, especially if it comes early in the wait."

– Paco Underhill, *Why We Buy*

Data Fields

Whether you are working in a large, technology-rich organization or in a smaller store that does things "by hand," it is equally important that you enter all information carefully, completely, and accurately. You need to become familiar with all of the sections on forms that must be completed (these are sometimes called "fields") and make sure you enter the right information for every transaction. Many retailers design their price tags to include the information that is also needed on the bill of sale; sales associates can then transfer the needed information from the price tag to the bill of sale. If scanners are used, the pertinent information is built into the barcode and sales associates will not have to handwrite or key in the information.

Tip: *It is a lot easier to remember to fill in all the necessary information if you know why it is important—learn as much as you can about your store's "behind-the-scenes" procedures.*

Here are just a few examples of how certain information recorded at the time of a transaction might used:

Type of Information Recorded	Possible Uses of Information
Name of Customer	➤ To record charges to in-store accounts ➤ To provide contact information for the sales associate ➤ To verify purchases when refunds are requested ➤ To track purchases for future target marketing
Item Number	➤ To update inventory records for reordering ➤ To track sales success of specific items ➤ To provide product information to customer for reorder or service needs
Department Name or Number	➤ To analyze success of department-specific promotions ➤ To track sales goals ➤ To complete financial statements
Item Description	➤ To verify purchases in case refunds are requested ➤ To track items put on layaway, sent to alterations, or special ordered

Type of Information Recorded	Possible Uses of Information
Date of Sale	➤ To update inventory records ➤ To analyze sales trends for future promotion activities ➤ To enforce refund or price adjustment policies
Price	➤ To calculate amount owed by customer ➤ To determine sales revenues ➤ To verify purchase price if refunds are requested ➤ To balance registers at the end of the day
Sales Associate Name or Number	➤ To track progress toward sales goals ➤ To award sales commissions ➤ To provide contact for customer
Method of Payment	➤ To aid in balancing the register at the end of the day ➤ To enforce refund or price adjustment policies ➤ To ensure proper processing of credit transactions

Handwritten Receipts

If your store requires you to complete a handwritten receipt or "bill of sale" for each transaction, check with your manager or a co-worker to make sure you know exactly what information must be included. Some stores will use standard forms and do not necessarily require that you fill in every field. Others will provide custom-designed forms and expect you to fill in each field in a very specific manner. Be sure you know the requirements for your store.

Tip: *Team up with a co-worker to speed up the transaction as you are completing the bill of sale. Co-workers can help by locating requested merchandise, packaging purchases, or reading item numbers to you as you enter the information.*

Sample of Handwritten Bill of Sale

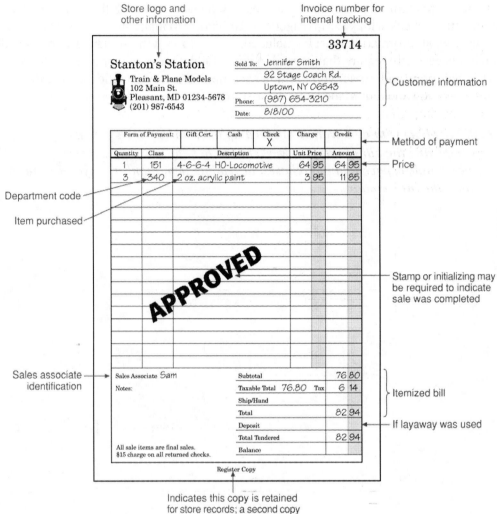

Store logo and other information

Invoice number for internal tracking

33714

Stanton's Station
Train & Plane Models
102 Main St.
Pleasant, MD 01234-5678
(201) 987-6543

Sold To: Jennifer Smith
92 Stage Coach Rd.
Uptown, NY 06543
Phone: (987) 654-3210
Date: 8/8/00

Customer information

Form of Payment:	Gift Cert.	Cash	Check	Charge	Credit
			X		

Method of payment

Quantity	Class	Description	Unit Price	Amount
1	151	4-6-6-4 HO-Locomotive	64 95	64 95
3	340	2 oz. acrylic paint	3 95	11 85

Price

Department code

Item purchased

APPROVED

Stamp or initializing may be required to indicate sale was completed

Sales associate identification

Sales Associate Sam
Notes:

Subtotal	76 80
Taxable Total 76.80 Tax	6 14
Ship/Hand	
Total	82 94
Deposit	
Total Tendered	82 94
Balance	

All sale items are final sales.
$15 charge on all returned checks.

Itemized bill

If layaway was used

Register Copy

Indicates this copy is retained for store records; a second copy would be given to the customer.

PERFECT PAPERWORK

Complete the bill of sale for the following scenario.

Your customer, Anton Young, is buying a pair of brown shoes today. The brand is Harry & Bill, the style is Classic Loafer #4, and the price is $94.99. Anton is also buying three pairs of socks at $7.00 each. The code for the men's shoe department is MSD and your employee number is D6. Anton is paying with cash. There is no sales tax.

NAME:

Chino's
Distinctive Men's Apparel

TEL.
New Customer _____ On List _____
Referred by _____
DATE _____ CLERK # _____

business office—
567 Dashing Place
Dapper, OH
01234-5678
(201) 555-3456

the store—
123 Sartorial Drive
Dapper, OH
01234-5678
(201) 555-6543

QTY.	DESCRIPTION	DEPT.	UNIT PRICE	TOTAL
			SUBTOTAL	
			SHIPPING CHARGES	
			SALES TAX	
			TOTAL	

Form of Payment: ☐ CASH ☐ CHECK ☐ CREDIT ☐ GIFT CERT. ☐ ACCOUNT
NOTES:

All sale items are final sales.
$15 charge on all returned checks.
No returns on evening wear, jewelry, hats, shoes, socks.

65740

Compare your completed bill of sale to the one in the Appendix.

P A R T 4

Wrap It Up!

32

Completing the Sales Transactions

Wrap It Up!

The first step as you prepare to send purchases home with the customer is to remove any security devices that your store may have attached to the merchandise. These devices, called Electronic Article Surveillance (EAS) tools are often used for higher-price items that are targeted by shoplifters. If the devices are not removed, an alarm will sound when the customer tries to leave the store. Another type of security device, often used by drugstores, contains a coded strip that must be deactivated with a scanning device or it, too, will set off alarms when the customer leaves the store. A third type of security device, often used on apparel, contains permanent dye that will stain merchandise if removed by anyone other than the sales associate.

While these are all helpful tools for preventing shoplifting, they can also be a source of embarrassment for customers if you forget to deactivate them after ringing up the sale. If a customer tries to leave the store with an item that has been paid for and an alarm sounds, you must react quickly and correct the mistake. If possible, go directly to the exit and accompany the customer back to the sales counter to remove or deactivate the security device. You should apologize quite publicly to help restore the customer's reputation with other shoppers. If you do not, that customer may always associate your store with this embarrassing incident and never return.

Tip: *Be sure that the tools that remove or deactivate the security device are kept secure. Quite often the device is chained or bolted in the checkout area.*

Packaging Merchandise Appropriately

You'll need to consider several things as you decide how to package purchases for the trip home with your customer. As you get ready to package items, consider:

> ➤ Is the item fragile? Will it break, bend, wrinkle, leak, or scratch?

> ➤ Are several items being purchased that should be separated from each other? (such as food and cleaning supplies, paper goods and liquids, or hot items and cold items)

> ➤ Are the purchases heavy or bulky? Should you separate them into more than one package?

> ➤ Is the item too big for normal packaging?

> ➤ Are there some very small items that might get lost?

> ➤ Is the item a gift?

Handle with care... Fragile items should always be wrapped individually. Materials suited for protecting fragile items include tissue paper, shredded paper, Styrofoam "popcorn," or individual boxes. Clothing should be folded neatly and also wrapped in tissue paper before being placed in a bag or box. Some clothing items should be left on the hanger and covered with a plastic bag, if your store allows. Even paper items should be handled with care and wrapped separately to keep them from getting bent or marred by other purchases.

Packaging Suggestions

Plants or flowers	Wrapped in kraft paper or placed in shallow box to prevent breakage during packaging
Fine fabrics	Left on hanger or individually wrapped in tissue paper
Pottery	Shredded packaging or kraft paper and sturdy box
Glassware	Foam wrap or tissue paper, in box with popcorn or cardboard dividers
Tiny individual items	Plastic self-sealing bags or paper bags taped closed to prevent scattering
Fresh produce, meat, or other items that might leak	Individual plastic bags

Prepare to be handled... If the purchases add up in weight, split them between two bags to make it easier for the customer to carry. Try to distribute the weight evenly and consider "double bagging" to ensure the bags will hold the weight of the merchandise. When bagging a variety of merchandise, place heavy items in the bottom of the bag and lighter or more fragile items on the top. Try to square-up the items in the bag so that the contents won't shift during the trip home. If an item is too large to fit in a bag, consider how you might make it easier for the customer to carry—you might create a handle using string or packaging tape wrapped all the way around a large box or the original carton.

As you package the merchandise, review the purchases with the customer just to be sure that everything is correct and the customer is aware of how the items are packed.

Sales Associate:	"I wrapped each glass individually and taped the tissue so it won't come loose before you get home."
Sales Associate:	"I've wrapped the blade of your knife in cardboard."
Sales Associate:	"Your cards are in a separate bag, inside next to the boxed items to keep them from bending."
Sales Associate:	"I put the nuts and bolts in a smaller bag and taped it closed. Is it okay if I load all of your other purchases into the bucket you are buying? I think it would be sturdier than a paper bag."

When an item is best left unpackaged (such as the bucket example above, or an item in its original carton with handles), be sure it is clear that the item has been paid for. Some stores have special tape or tags to use as proof of purchase. If not, you can at least tape the receipt to the item in plain sight to help the customer get out of the store without being stopped.

Tip: *If shoppers have lots of packages (even from other stores), offer a larger shopping bag with a handle to consolidate their purchases.*

The Art of Gift Giving

Gift purchases usually require some special handling. When you know the item is a gift, offer to remove the price tags. If the customer is concerned about the item being returnable, explain your store's policy. Some stores will issue gift receipts on which the purchase price is disguised. Some stores write the purchase price and date in "code" on the tags. These techniques allow the person receiving the item to return it easily and get full value for their exchange. If your store offers gift wrapping services, be sure to tell the customer this and explain any charges. At a minimum, offer a gift box (if available) and let the customer know if your store sells gift wrapping materials or cards.

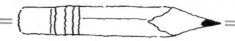

A CLEAN GETAWAY

Describe how you would wrap the following purchases so customers could easily and safely transport them home. We've done the first one for you.

Sweater

Fold neatly, wrap in tissue paper, and place in bag. This will help keep the sweater clean and prevent it from being snagged by other purchases.

Necklace and a pair of earrings

_____

_____

Set of six glasses

_____

_____

Large wash bucket, detergent, sponges, and rubber gloves

_____

_____

Tapered candles, glass candleholders, and gift card

_____

_____

Bicycle, already assembled

_____

_____

Box of crackers, two cans of soup, bottle of syrup, loaf of bread, and bunch of five bananas

_____

_____

_____

Compare your responses to the suggestions in the back of the Appendix.

Would You Like Some Help with That?

Would You Like Some Help with That?

Customers will appreciate the care you have taken to package their purchases carefully. Now that they are ready to take home their treasures, you may be able to offer some final service to make that trip easier.

Carry your bags, sir?...If customers have several bags or some heavy or bulky items, you might offer to carry packages to their car or arrange for someone else to do it. You might tie boxes together and attach a handle to make it easier to carry. You could also arrange for customers to retrieve their items at a package pickup area. Be sure to explain any procedures or paperwork and the location of the pickup area.

Sales Associate: "This package is kind of heavy. Would you like some help out with it?"

Sales Associate: "I will have your television waiting for you at Package Pick-Up at the northeast corner of the store. Just honk your horn and someone will come out to help you. You'll need to show them this receipt."

Sales Associate: "These boxes aren't heavy, but carrying three will be awkward. May I tie them together with twine so they'll be easier for you to carry?"

Tip: *You should be thanking the customer, not the other way around. The most important lesson in closing the sale: Always say thank you!*

Would You Like That Delivered?

Another way to lighten the load for shoppers is to offer to have their purchases delivered. This service is quite common for drugstores, florists, lumber and hardware stores, lawn and garden centers or nurseries, and major appliance dealers. Other retailers are finding ways to add this service to build customer loyalty. Whether the merchandise is being delivered to the customer or being sent as a gift, the customer needs to be assured that it will arrive at its destination safely and on time. As a sales associate, your job is to:

➤ Make customers aware of delivery services if available

➤ Explain delivery options (courier, postal service, or store-operated service)

➤ Explain any charges or other requirements

➤ Obtain all necessary information from the customer

➤ Arrange for acceptable delivery date and times

➤ Complete all paperwork for the delivery request

➤ Write clearly and neatly

➤ Pack merchandise carefully for shipment

➤ Follow up to make sure delivery was completed to customers' satisfaction

A taxing question... If your store normally charges sales tax (this will vary by state and sometimes by type of merchandise), there may be exceptions if you are shipping to another state. If your company does not have a retail outlet in the state you are shipping to, the customer should not be charged your state's sales tax. Your store should have a list of such sales tax exemptions; refer to this list as you prepare the delivery order.

Shipping it to the shipping department... Some stores have a shipping department; in other stores, the sales associates must fill out the paperwork and prepare purchases to be delivered. If your company has a shipping department, you will probably still have to get all of the necessary information from the customer to pass along. If your store's procedure is to have the customer complete a delivery request form, you should check the completed form carefully to make sure all the information is there and that it is readable.

If you are writing the information yourself, print carefully and then show the completed form to the customer and ask if it is all correct. In addition to handling the paperwork correctly, you must take care with the purchases and make sure that the items to be delivered do not get separated from the shipping information. One method is to put the customer's purchases in a shopping bag and staple the delivery information to the bag before handing it off to the shipping department.

Shipping it yourself... If you are preparing the purchases for shipment yourself, you will need to pack the items carefully, according to your store's guidelines. You will also need to understand any charges established by your store or by the vendor who handles your deliveries. Some stores will allow customers to select how they want their purchases shipped; other stores may have a contract with just one shipping vendor or have their own local delivery service.

Tip: *Make a note on the delivery order of any special situations. If a mattress has to be carried up several flights of stairs, more than one delivery person may be needed!*

You will need to learn how to read the delivery fee schedule. This will tell you how much to charge for delivering each item depending on its weight, dimensions, distance it is to be shipped, and urgency of delivery. Generally, the faster it is delivered, the more it will cost. When customers request a "rush" delivery, be sure they understand any extra charges involved. Here is an example of a very simple shipping fee schedule that might be used by a sales associate to determine delivery charges:

Fee Schedule for Shipping from Store 1			
	Zone 1	**Zone 2**	**Zone 3**
Destination Zip Codes	90000	60000-89999	10000-59999
Economy Delivery (allow 5 days)			
up to 5 pounds	$3.00	$4.00	$ 5.00
5 to 10 pounds	$5.00	$6.00	$ 7.00
over 10 pounds	$8.00	$9.00	$10.00
Rush Delivery (allow 2 days)			
up to 5 pounds	$5.00	$6.00	$7.00
5 to 10 pounds	$7.00	$8.00	$9.00
over 10 pounds	$9.00	$11.00	$12.00
Overnight Delivery (allow 24 hours)			
up to 5 pounds	$10.00	$10.00	$10.00
5 to 10 pounds	$15.00	$15.00	$15.00
over 10 pounds	$20.00	$20.00	$20.00
NOTE: add $5.00 handling fee to all delivery orders			

Keep a copy of all shipping records, at least until you are confident that the customer has received the item and is satisfied with the purchase. Remember, in the customers' eyes, you are the store, and they will seek you out if they have any questions about their delivery. By keeping copies of the shipping records, you will be prepared to help them.

A Final Good Impression

> *Ask the customer to come back and make sure you have given him or her good reason to do so.*"

–Don Taylor and Jeanne Smalling Archer,
Up Against the Wal-Marts

If your store is planning a special promotion in the near future, be sure to mention it as you close the sale. Most customers will appreciate the advance notice. If you have free samples or coupons to give away, don't just drop them in the bag; mention the gift as you place it in the shopping bag. Use these opportunities to remind customers how much you value them and look forward to seeing them again in the future. And don't forget the last words customers should hear from you before they leave…

"Thank you for shopping with us today!"

PREPARING FOR SHIPSHAPE DELIVERIES

Using the shipping fee schedule earlier in this chapter, complete the delivery order for the following scenario.

The customer, Madeline Roberts, likes to buy gifts for her out-of-state friends and relatives from your store because it is locally owned, is one-of-a-kind, and carries items that cannot be found anywhere else.

Madeline has purchased a $45.00 shirt for a cross-country relative. She would like it gift wrapped and has signed a card to be included. Your store does not charge for gift wrap, but does normally charge 10% sales tax. Madeline is paying with a personal check and her phone number is (425) 868-5599.

Madeline would like the gift sent to Billy Roberts, 124 Elm Street, Apt. 22, New York, NY 10333. This is Zone 3 on the fee schedule shown on the shipping fee schedule. Billy's phone number is (222) 938-5115. His birthday is in three days and the package must arrive by then.

CONTINUED

Delivery Request Form
Pacific Gear

0753

Date _____

Method of Delivery:

❏ Economy   ❏ Rush   ❏ Overnight

Ship to:

Receiver's name _____

Address _____ Apt. _____

City _____ State _____ Zip _____

Phone (   ) _____

Special Instructions: _____

_____

Ship From:

Sender _____ Phone _____

Sold by _____ Store# _____

Item(s) _____

_____

Purchase Price _____

_____

Tax _____

Shipping & handling _____

Total _____

Method of Payment:

❏ Cash   ❏ Check   ❏ Bank card

❏ Store account   ❏ Other _____

Compare your answers to those in the Appendix.

A P P E N D I X

Roundup: Completing the Sales Transaction

The following is a brief roundup of concepts of completing the transaction that you have explored in this workbook. Check (✓) the items that you now feel prepared to accomplish as a sales associate.

- ❏ Handle transactions and related paperwork

- ❏ Open, maintain, and close the cash register

- ❏ Package merchandise appropriately

- ❏ Assure that shipping/mailing/deliveries are handled properly

If you were unable to check one or more of the items listed above, review the pages related to those topics. And remember that you will be able to refine and improve all of these skills as you build customer relationships on the job. The more confident you are with customers, the more satisfied they will be.

Learning Checklist for Workbook 8

As you complete the workbook *Completing the Sales Transaction,* record your progress using the following checklists. These checklists can also be used as a basis for discussion with your instructor, supervisor, or mentor as you complete the skill practices and/or you demonstrate the specific skills in the workplace.

Lessons completed   **Date completed**

❑   Will That Be Cash?   _____

❑   Accepting Checks and Credit Cards   _____

❑   Completing the Paperwork   _____

❑   Wrap It Up!   _____

❑   Would You Like Some Help with That?   _____

**Skills Demonstrated
in the Workplace**

❏ Handle transactions and related paperwork   _____

Describe the situation and how you demonstrated this skill:

_____

_____

_____

❏ Open, maintain, and close the cash register   _____

Describe the situation and how you demonstrated this skill:

_____

_____

_____

❏ Package merchandise appropriately   _____

Describe the situation and how you demonstrated this skill:

_____

_____

_____

❏ Assure that shipping/mailing/deliveries are handled properly   _____

Describe the situation and how you demonstrated this skill:

_____

_____

_____

Appendix to Part 1

Comments & Suggested Responses

Now You Figure It Out

1. The amount due is $33.17 and the customer gives you $35. What kind of change does the customer receive back?

$33.17	+	**.01**	**(penny)**	=	**33.18**
$33.18	+	.01		=	33.19
$33.19	+	.01		=	33.20
$33.20	+	.05	(nickel)	=	33.25
$33.25	+	.25	(quarter)	=	33.50
$33.50	+	.25		=	33.75
$33.75	+	.25		=	34.00
$34.00	+	1.00	(dollar)	=	35.00

You give the customer: **3 pennies, 1 nickel, 3 quarters, and 1 one-dollar bill.**

2. The amount due is $234.68 and the customer gives you $300.00. What kind of change does the customer receive back?

$234.68	+	.01	(penny)	=	234.69	
$234.69	+	.01		=	234.70	
$234.70	+	.05	(nickel)	=	234.75	
$234.75	+	.25	(quarter)	=	235.00	
$235.00	+	5.00	($5 bill)	=	240.00	
$240.00	+	20.00	($20 bill)	=	260.00	Option
$260.00	+	20.00		=	280.00	240.00 + 10.00 = 250.00
$280.00	+	20.00		=	**300.00**	250.00 + 50.00 = 300.00

You give the customer: 2 pennies, 1 nickel, 1 quarter, 1 five-dollar bill, and 3 twenty-dollar bills.

or

2 pennies, 1 nickel, 1 quarter, 1 five-dollar bill, 1 ten-dollar bill, and 1 fifty-dollar bill.

3. The amount due is $51.25 and the customer gives you 3 twenty-dollar bills, 1 one-dollar bill, and 1 quarter.

How much money did the customer give you? $61.25

What kind of change does the customer receive back?

$51.25   +   10.00 ($10 bill)   = $61.25

You give the customer: 1 ten-dollar bill (or 2 five-dollar bills; or 10 one-dollar bills)

Appendix to Part 2

Comments & Suggested Responses

Do These Check Out?

Some mistakes that you should watch for when accepting checks are noted on these examples.

Amounts do not match

Missing date

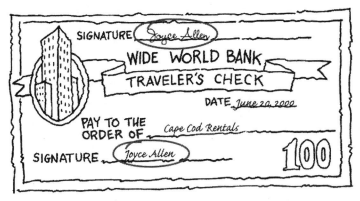

JOSEPH DOUGH   2988
SMALL CHANGE AVE.
NEW YORK, N.Y.   DATE April 14, 2000

PAY TO THE
ORDER OF _Linda's Oil Lamps_ $ 10.40
        Ten and 40/100

BUCKAROO BANK
NEW YORK, N.Y.   Joseph B. Broke

Signature does not match printed name

SIGNATURE   Joyce Allen
            WIDE WORLD BANK
            TRAVELER'S CHECK
                    DATE June 20, 2000
PAY TO THE
ORDER OF   Cape Cod Rentals
SIGNATURE   Joyce Allen   100

Signatures do not match

Appendix to Part 3

Comments & Suggested Responses

Perfect Paperwork

Your completed bill of sale should look like this.

QTY.	DESCRIPTION	DEPT.	UNIT PRICE	TOTAL
1	Harry & Bill classic	MSD		
	loafer #4 (brown)		94.99	94.99
3	socks	MSD	7.00	21.00

NAME: Anton Young

Chino's
Distinctive Men's Apparel

TEL.
New Customer ____ On List ____
Referred by ____
DATE 8-30-99   CLERK # D6

business office—
567 Dashing Place
Dapper, OH
01234-5678
(201) 555-3456

the store—
123 Sartorial Drive
Dapper, OH
01234-5678
(201) 555-6543

SUBTOTAL	115.99
SHIPPING CHARGES	
SALES TAX	
TOTAL	115.99

Form of Payment: ✔ CASH ☐ CHECK ☐ CREDIT ☐ GIFT CERT. ☐ ACCOUNT
NOTES:

All sale items are final sales.
$15 charge on all returned checks.
No returns on evening wear, jewelry, hats, shoes, socks.

65740

Appendix to Part 4

Comments & Suggested Responses

A Clean Getaway

Here are some ideas for wrapping purchases so customers get them home easily and safely. Your answers may be slightly different, but review these suggestions for any special tips you might not have considered.

Necklace and a pair of earrings

> The best approach would be to put the necklace in one small box and the earrings in another, to prevent them from getting tangled or scratching each other. If the boxes do not have cotton padding, consider wrapping the items in tissue first.

Set of six glasses

> Wrap each glass individually in tissue or foam wrap. Arrange them in a sturdy box, one with cardboard dividers if available, to prevent breakage.

Large wash bucket, detergent, sponges, and rubber gloves

> Put all items inside the bucket, if this is acceptable to the customer. The bucket will probably be easier to carry by its handle, and putting all items inside means the customer has only one package to carry. Be sure to use some technique to indicate that the items have been paid for.

Tapered candles, glass candleholders, and gift card

> Provide a gift box, if possible. At a minimum, wrap each individual item securely in tissue paper and place the candles on top of the candleholders or in a separate bag so they won't be broken by the heavier candleholders.

Bicycle, already assembled

> Tag the item before the customer wheels it out of the store so that others will know it is paid for.

Box of crackers, two cans of soup, bottle of syrup, loaf of bread, and bunch of five bananas

> Use a flat-bottom paper bag and put the crackers at one end of the bottom of the bag, the cans of soup at the other. Put the syrup in a plastic bag and place it between the soup and crackers on the bottom. This keeps the items from shifting and protects the crackers from the cans. Place the bananas on top of the soup cans and the bread across the top of all other items so it won't get squished.

Appendix to Part 5

Comments & Suggested Responses

Preparing for Shipshape Deliveries

Using the shipping fee schedule in this chapter, you would have determined that Madeline's relative lives in Zone 3 and that the gift will have to be delivered using Rush service to get there in time. It is safe to assume that a shirt, even wrapped and packaged, is not going to weigh more than 5 pounds. Therefore the shipping fee is $7.00 plus the $5.00 handling fee noted at the bottom of the chart. Total delivery cost = $12.00.

Fee Schedule for Shipping from Store 1			
	Zone 1	**Zone 2**	**Zone 3**
Destination Zip Codes	90000	60000-89999	10000-59999
Economy Delivery (allow 5 days)			
up to 5 pounds	$3.00	$4.00	$ 5.00
5 to 10 pounds	$5.00	$6.00	$ 7.00
over 10 pounds	$8.00	$9.00	$10.00
Rush Delivery (allow 2 days)			
up to 5 pounds	$5.00	$6.00	$7.00
5 to 10 pounds	$7.00	$8.00	$9.00
over 10 pounds	$9.00	$11.00	$12.00
Overnight Delivery (allow 24 hours)			
up to 5 pounds	$10.00	$10.00	$10.00
5 to 10 pounds	$15.00	$15.00	$15.00
over 10 pounds	$20.00	$20.00	$20.00
NOTE: add $5.00 handling fee to all delivery orders			

Your completed Delivery Request Form should look like this:

Delivery Request Form
Pacific Gear

0753

Date _8/8/00_

Method of Delivery:

❑ Economy   ☒ Rush   ❑ Overnight

Ship to:

Receiver's name _Billy Roberts_
Address _124 Elm St_   Apt. _22_
City _New York_   State _NY_ Zip _10333_
Phone (_222_) _868-5599_
Special Instructions: _Gift wrap and include card provided_
by customer.

Ship From:

Sender _Madeline Roberts_   Phone _(987) 654-3210_
Sold by _your name_   Store# _1_
Item(s) _shirt_

Purchase Price $45.00

Tax   0
Shipping & handling _($7 shipping & $5 handling)_ $12.00
Total $57.00

Method of Payment:

❑ Cash   ☒ Check   ❑ Bank card
❑ Store account   ❑ Other _____

NOTES

NOTES

NOTES

NOTES

NOTES

NOTES

Also Available

Books • Videos • CD-ROMs • Computer-Based Training Products

If you enjoyed this book, we have great news for you. There are more than 200 books available in the *Crisp Fifty-Minute™ Series*. For more information visit us online at

www.courseilt.com

Subject Areas Include:

Management

Human Resources

Communication Skills

Personal Development

Sales/Marketing

Finance

Coaching and Mentoring

Customer Service/Quality

Small Business and Entrepreneurship

Training

Life Planning

Writing

VERP